Project to complete

I0505327

project	
deadline	completed ☐

items required | tasks to-do

project	
deadline	completed ☐

items required | tasks to-do

Project to complete

project	
deadline	completed ☐

items required

tasks to-do

project	
deadline	completed ☐

items required

tasks to-do

Project to complete

project	
deadline	completed ☐

items required

tasks to-do

project	
deadline	completed ☐

items required

tasks to-do

Project to complete

project	
deadline	completed ☐

items required

tasks to-do

project	
deadline	completed ☐

items required

tasks to-do

Project to complete

project	
deadline	completed ☐

items required

tasks to-do

project	
deadline	completed ☐

items required

tasks to-do

Project to complete

project	
deadline	completed ☐

items required

☐
☐
☐
☐
☐
☐

tasks to-do

☐
☐
☐
☐
☐

project	
deadline	completed ☐

items required

☐
☐
☐
☐
☐
☐

tasks to-do

☐
☐
☐
☐
☐

Project to complete

project	
deadline	completed ☐

items required

tasks to-do

project	
deadline	completed ☐

items required

tasks to-do

Project to complete

project	
deadline	completed ☐

items required

☐ _____
☐ _____
☐ _____
☐ _____
☐ _____
☐ _____

tasks to-do

☐ _____
☐ _____
☐ _____
☐ _____
☐ _____
☐ _____

_____
_____
_____
_____
_____

project	
deadline	completed ☐

items required

☐ _____
☐ _____
☐ _____
☐ _____
☐ _____
☐ _____

tasks to-do

☐ _____
☐ _____
☐ _____
☐ _____
☐ _____
☐ _____

_____
_____
_____
_____
_____

Project to complete

project	
deadline	completed ☐

items required   tasks to-do

project	
deadline	completed ☐

items required   tasks to-do

Project to complete

project	
deadline	completed ☐

items required

☐ _____
☐ _____
☐ _____
☐ _____
☐ _____
☐ _____

tasks to-do

☐ _____
☐ _____
☐ _____
☐ _____
☐ _____
☐ _____

_____
_____
_____
_____
_____

project	
deadline	completed ☐

items required

☐ _____
☐ _____
☐ _____
☐ _____
☐ _____
☐ _____

tasks to-do

☐ _____
☐ _____
☐ _____
☐ _____
☐ _____
☐ _____

_____
_____
_____
_____
_____

Project to complete

project	
deadline	completed ☐

items required

tasks to-do

project	
deadline	completed ☐

items required

tasks to-do

Project to complete

project	
deadline	completed ☐

items required

☐
☐
☐
☐
☐
☐

tasks to-do

☐
☐
☐
☐
☐
☐

project	
deadline	completed ☐

items required

☐
☐
☐
☐
☐
☐

tasks to-do

☐
☐
☐
☐
☐
☐

Project to complete

project	
deadline	completed ☐

items required

tasks to-do

- ☐
- ☐
- ☐
- ☐
- ☐
- ☐

- ☐
- ☐
- ☐
- ☐
- ☐

project	
deadline	completed ☐

items required

tasks to-do

- ☐
- ☐
- ☐
- ☐
- ☐
- ☐

- ☐
- ☐
- ☐
- ☐
- ☐

Project to complete

project	
deadline	completed ☐

items required   tasks to-do

☐
☐
☐
☐
☐
☐

☐
☐
☐
☐
☐

project	
deadline	completed ☐

items required   tasks to-do

☐
☐
☐
☐
☐
☐

☐
☐
☐
☐
☐

Project to complete

project	
deadline	completed ☐

items required

tasks to-do

project	
deadline	completed ☐

items required

tasks to-do

Project to complete

project	
deadline	completed ☐

items required

- ☐
- ☐
- ☐
- ☐
- ☐
- ☐

tasks to-do

- ☐
- ☐
- ☐
- ☐
- ☐
- ☐

project	
deadline	completed ☐

items required

- ☐
- ☐
- ☐
- ☐
- ☐
- ☐

tasks to-do

- ☐
- ☐
- ☐
- ☐
- ☐
- ☐

Project to complete

project	
deadline	completed ☐

items required

tasks to-do

project	
deadline	completed ☐

items required

tasks to-do

Project to complete

project	
deadline	completed ☐

items required

tasks to-do

project	
deadline	completed ☐

items required

tasks to-do

Project to complete

project	
deadline	completed ☐

items required

tasks to-do

project	
deadline	completed ☐

items required

tasks to-do

Project to complete

project	
deadline	completed ☐

items required

tasks to-do

project	
deadline	completed ☐

items required

tasks to-do

Project to complete

project	
deadline	completed ☐

items required	tasks to-do
☐	☐
☐	☐
☐	☐
☐	☐
☐	☐
☐	☐

project	
deadline	completed ☐

items required	tasks to-do
☐	☐
☐	☐
☐	☐
☐	☐
☐	☐
☐	☐

Project to complete

project	
deadline	completed ☐

items required | tasks to-do

Project to complete

project	
deadline	completed ☐

items required   tasks to-do

project	
deadline	completed ☐

items required   tasks to-do

Project to complete

project	
deadline	completed ☐

items required

tasks to-do

project	
deadline	completed ☐

items required

tasks to-do

Project to complete

project	
deadline	completed ☐

items required

tasks to-do

☐
☐
☐
☐
☐
☐

☐
☐
☐
☐
☐
☐

project	
deadline	completed ☐

items required

tasks to-do

☐
☐
☐
☐
☐
☐

☐
☐
☐
☐
☐
☐

Project to complete

project	
deadline	completed ☐

items required

tasks to-do

project	
deadline	completed ☐

items required

tasks to-do

Project to complete

project	
deadline	completed ☐

items required

☐
☐
☐
☐
☐
☐

tasks to-do

☐
☐
☐
☐
☐

project	
deadline	completed ☐

items required

☐
☐
☐
☐
☐
☐

tasks to-do

☐
☐
☐
☐
☐

Project to complete

project	
deadline	completed ☐

items required

tasks to-do

project	
deadline	completed ☐

items required

tasks to-do

Project to complete

project	
deadline	completed ☐

items required

tasks to-do

project	
deadline	completed ☐

items required

tasks to-do

Project to complete

project	
deadline	completed ☐

items required

- ☐
- ☐
- ☐
- ☐
- ☐
- ☐

tasks to-do

- ☐
- ☐
- ☐
- ☐
- ☐
- ☐

project	
deadline	completed ☐

items required

- ☐
- ☐
- ☐
- ☐
- ☐
- ☐

tasks to-do

- ☐
- ☐
- ☐
- ☐
- ☐
- ☐

Project to complete

project	
deadline	completed ☐

items required

☐
☐
☐
☐
☐
☐

tasks to-do

☐
☐
☐
☐
☐
☐

project	
deadline	completed ☐

items required

☐
☐
☐
☐
☐
☐

tasks to-do

☐
☐
☐
☐
☐
☐

Project to complete

project	
deadline	completed ☐

items required

tasks to-do

project	
deadline	completed ☐

items required

tasks to-do

Project to complete

project	
deadline	completed ☐

items required

tasks to-do

project	
deadline	completed ☐

items required

tasks to-do

Project to complete

project	
deadline	completed ☐

items required

tasks to-do

---

project	
deadline	completed ☐

items required

tasks to-do

Project to complete

project	
deadline	completed ☐

items required

tasks to-do

project	
deadline	completed ☐

items required

tasks to-do

Project to complete

project	
deadline	completed ☐

items required

☐ _____
☐ _____
☐ _____
☐ _____
☐ _____
☐ _____

tasks to-do

☐ _____
☐ _____
☐ _____
☐ _____
☐ _____
☐ _____

_____
_____
_____
_____
_____

project	
deadline	completed ☐

items required

☐ _____
☐ _____
☐ _____
☐ _____
☐ _____
☐ _____

tasks to-do

☐ _____
☐ _____
☐ _____
☐ _____
☐ _____

_____
_____
_____
_____
_____

Project to complete

project	
deadline	completed ☐

items required

tasks to-do

project	
deadline	completed ☐

items required

tasks to-do

Project to complete

project	
deadline	completed ☐

items required

tasks to-do

project	
deadline	completed ☐

items required

tasks to-do

Project to complete

project	
deadline	completed ☐

items required

tasks to-do

project	
deadline	completed ☐

items required

tasks to-do

Project to complete

project	
deadline	completed ☐

items required

tasks to-do

project	
deadline	completed ☐

items required

tasks to-do

Project to complete

project	
deadline	completed ☐

items required

tasks to-do

project	
deadline	completed ☐

items required

tasks to-do

Project to complete

project	
deadline	completed ☐

items required

☐ _____
☐ _____
☐ _____
☐ _____
☐ _____
☐ _____

tasks to-do

☐ _____
☐ _____
☐ _____
☐ _____
☐ _____
☐ _____

_____
_____
_____
_____
_____
_____

project	
deadline	completed ☐

items required

☐ _____
☐ _____
☐ _____
☐ _____
☐ _____
☐ _____

tasks to-do

☐ _____
☐ _____
☐ _____
☐ _____
☐ _____

_____
_____
_____
_____
_____
_____

Project to complete

project	
deadline	completed ☐

items required

tasks to-do

project	
deadline	completed ☐

items required

tasks to-do

Project to complete

project	
deadline	completed ☐

items required

tasks to-do

project	
deadline	completed ☐

items required

tasks to-do

Project to complete

project	
deadline	completed ☐

items required

tasks to-do

project	
deadline	completed ☐

items required

tasks to-do

Project to complete

project	
deadline	completed ☐

items required

☐
☐
☐
☐
☐
☐

tasks to-do

☐
☐
☐
☐
☐

project	
deadline	completed ☐

items required

☐
☐
☐
☐
☐
☐

tasks to-do

☐
☐
☐
☐
☐

Project to complete

project	
deadline	completed ☐

items required

tasks to-do

- ☐
- ☐
- ☐
- ☐
- ☐
- ☐

- ☐
- ☐
- ☐
- ☐
- ☐
- ☐

project	
deadline	completed ☐

items required

tasks to-do

- ☐
- ☐
- ☐
- ☐
- ☐
- ☐

- ☐
- ☐
- ☐
- ☐
- ☐
- ☐

Project to complete

project	
deadline	completed ☐

items required

tasks to-do

project	
deadline	completed ☐

items required

tasks to-do

Project to complete

project	
deadline	completed ☐

items required

tasks to-do

project	
deadline	completed ☐

items required

tasks to-do

Project to complete

project	
deadline	completed ☐

items required

tasks to-do

project	
deadline	completed ☐

items required

tasks to-do

Project to complete

project	
deadline	completed ☐

items required

tasks to-do

project	
deadline	completed ☐

items required

tasks to-do

Project to complete

project	
deadline	completed ☐

items required

☐
☐
☐
☐
☐
☐

tasks to-do

☐
☐
☐
☐
☐
☐

project	
deadline	completed ☐

items required

☐
☐
☐
☐
☐
☐

tasks to-do

☐
☐
☐
☐
☐
☐

Project to complete

project	
deadline	completed ☐

items required

- ☐
- ☐
- ☐
- ☐
- ☐
- ☐

tasks to-do

- ☐
- ☐
- ☐
- ☐
- ☐
- ☐

project	
deadline	completed ☐

items required

- ☐
- ☐
- ☐
- ☐
- ☐
- ☐

tasks to-do

- ☐
- ☐
- ☐
- ☐
- ☐
- ☐

Project to complete

project	
deadline	completed ☐

items required

tasks to-do

project	
deadline	completed ☐

items required

tasks to-do

Project to complete

project	
deadline	completed ☐

items required

tasks to-do

project	
deadline	completed ☐

items required

tasks to-do

Project to complete

project	
deadline	completed ☐

items required

☐
☐
☐
☐
☐
☐

tasks to-do

☐
☐
☐
☐
☐

project	
deadline	completed ☐

items required

☐
☐
☐
☐
☐
☐

tasks to-do

☐
☐
☐
☐
☐

Project to complete

project	
deadline	completed ☐

items required

tasks to-do

project	
deadline	completed ☐

items required

tasks to-do

Project to complete

project	
deadline	completed ☐

items required

tasks to-do

project	
deadline	completed ☐

items required

tasks to-do

Project to complete

project	
deadline	completed ☐

items required

tasks to-do

project	
deadline	completed ☐

items required

tasks to-do

Project to complete

project	
deadline	completed ☐

items required

tasks to-do

project	
deadline	completed ☐

items required

tasks to-do

Project to complete

project	
deadline	completed ☐

items required

☐ _____
☐ _____
☐ _____
☐ _____
☐ _____
☐ _____

tasks to-do

☐ _____
☐ _____
☐ _____
☐ _____
☐ _____
☐ _____

_____
_____
_____
_____
_____

project	
deadline	completed ☐

items required

☐ _____
☐ _____
☐ _____
☐ _____
☐ _____
☐ _____

tasks to-do

☐ _____
☐ _____
☐ _____
☐ _____
☐ _____
☐ _____

_____
_____
_____
_____
_____

Project to complete

project	
deadline	completed ☐

items required

☐
☐
☐
☐
☐
☐

tasks to-do

☐
☐
☐
☐
☐
☐

project	
deadline	completed ☐

items required

☐
☐
☐
☐
☐
☐

tasks to-do

☐
☐
☐
☐
☐
☐

Project to complete

project	
deadline	completed ☐

items required   tasks to-do

project	
deadline	completed ☐

items required   tasks to-do

Project to complete

project	
deadline	completed ☐

items required

☐
☐
☐
☐
☐
☐

tasks to-do

☐
☐
☐
☐
☐
☐

project	
deadline	completed ☐

items required

☐
☐
☐
☐
☐
☐

tasks to-do

☐
☐
☐
☐
☐
☐

Project to complete

project	
deadline	completed ☐

items required

- ☐
- ☐
- ☐
- ☐
- ☐
- ☐

tasks to-do

- ☐
- ☐
- ☐
- ☐
- ☐
- ☐

project	
deadline	completed ☐

items required

- ☐
- ☐
- ☐
- ☐
- ☐
- ☐

tasks to-do

- ☐
- ☐
- ☐
- ☐
- ☐
- ☐

Project to complete

project	
deadline	completed ☐

items required

☐
☐
☐
☐
☐
☐

tasks to-do

☐
☐
☐
☐
☐
☐

project	
deadline	completed ☐

items required

☐
☐
☐
☐
☐
☐

tasks to-do

☐
☐
☐
☐
☐
☐

Project to complete

project	
deadline	completed ☐

items required

tasks to-do

project	
deadline	completed ☐

items required

tasks to-do

Project to complete

project	
deadline	completed ☐

items required

tasks to-do

project	
deadline	completed ☐

items required

tasks to-do

Project to complete

project	
deadline	completed ☐

items required	tasks to-do
☐	☐
☐	☐
☐	☐
☐	☐
☐	☐
☐	☐

project	
deadline	completed ☐

items required	tasks to-do
☐	☐
☐	☐
☐	☐
☐	☐
☐	☐
☐	☐

Project to complete

project	
deadline	completed ☐

items required

tasks to-do

project	
deadline	completed ☐

items required

tasks to-do

Project to complete

project	
deadline	completed ☐

items required

tasks to-do

project	
deadline	completed ☐

items required

tasks to-do

Project to complete

project	
deadline	completed ☐

items required

tasks to-do

project	
deadline	completed ☐

items required

tasks to-do

Project to complete

project	
deadline	completed ☐

items required

tasks to-do

project	
deadline	completed ☐

items required

tasks to-do

Project to complete

project	
deadline	completed ☐

items required

- ☐
- ☐
- ☐
- ☐
- ☐
- ☐

tasks to-do

- ☐
- ☐
- ☐
- ☐
- ☐

project	
deadline	completed ☐

items required

- ☐
- ☐
- ☐
- ☐
- ☐
- ☐

tasks to-do

- ☐
- ☐
- ☐
- ☐
- ☐

Project to complete

project	
deadline	completed ☐

items required

☐
☐
☐
☐
☐
☐

tasks to-do

☐
☐
☐
☐
☐

project	
deadline	completed ☐

items required

☐
☐
☐
☐
☐
☐

tasks to-do

☐
☐
☐
☐
☐

Project to complete

project	
deadline	completed ☐

items required

☐ _____
☐ _____
☐ _____
☐ _____
☐ _____
☐ _____

tasks to-do

☐ _____
☐ _____
☐ _____
☐ _____
☐ _____
☐ _____

_____
_____
_____
_____
_____

project	
deadline	completed ☐

items required

☐ _____
☐ _____
☐ _____
☐ _____
☐ _____
☐ _____

tasks to-do

☐ _____
☐ _____
☐ _____
☐ _____
☐ _____
☐ _____

_____
_____
_____
_____
_____

Project to complete

project	
deadline	completed ☐

items required

tasks to-do

project	
deadline	completed ☐

items required

tasks to-do

Project to complete

project	
deadline	completed ☐

items required

tasks to-do

---

project	
deadline	completed ☐

items required

tasks to-do

Project to complete

project	
deadline	completed ☐

items required

tasks to-do

project	
deadline	completed ☐

items required

tasks to-do

Project to complete

project	
deadline	completed ☐

items required

tasks to-do

project	
deadline	completed ☐

items required

tasks to-do

Project to complete

project	
deadline	completed ☐

items required tasks to-do

completed ☐

project	
deadline	completed ☐

items required tasks to-do

Project to complete

project	
deadline	completed ☐

items required

tasks to-do

project	
deadline	completed ☐

items required

tasks to-do

Project to complete

project	
deadline	completed ☐

items required | tasks to-do

project	
deadline	completed ☐

items required | tasks to-do

Project to complete

project	
deadline	completed ☐

items required

☐
☐
☐
☐
☐
☐

tasks to-do

☐
☐
☐
☐
☐
☐

project	
deadline	completed ☐

items required

☐
☐
☐
☐
☐
☐

tasks to-do

☐
☐
☐
☐
☐
☐

Project to complete

project	
deadline	completed ☐

items required

☐
☐
☐
☐
☐
☐

tasks to-do

☐
☐
☐
☐
☐

project	
deadline	completed ☐

items required

☐
☐
☐
☐
☐
☐

tasks to-do

☐
☐
☐
☐
☐

Project to complete

project	
deadline	completed ☐

items required

- ☐
- ☐
- ☐
- ☐
- ☐
- ☐

tasks to-do

- ☐
- ☐
- ☐
- ☐
- ☐
- ☐

project	
deadline	completed ☐

items required

- ☐
- ☐
- ☐
- ☐
- ☐
- ☐

tasks to-do

- ☐
- ☐
- ☐
- ☐
- ☐
- ☐

Project to complete

project	
deadline	completed ☐

items required

tasks to-do

project	
deadline	completed ☐

items required

tasks to-do

Project to complete

project	
deadline	completed ☐

items required

tasks to-do

project	
deadline	completed ☐

items required

tasks to-do

Project to complete

project	
deadline	completed ☐

items required

- ☐
- ☐
- ☐
- ☐
- ☐
- ☐

tasks to-do

- ☐
- ☐
- ☐
- ☐
- ☐

project	
deadline	completed ☐

items required

- ☐
- ☐
- ☐
- ☐
- ☐
- ☐

tasks to-do

- ☐
- ☐
- ☐
- ☐
- ☐
- ☐

Project to complete

project	
deadline	completed ☐

items required

tasks to-do

project	
deadline	completed ☐

items required

tasks to-do

Project to complete

project	
deadline	completed ☐

items required

☐ _____
☐ _____
☐ _____
☐ _____
☐ _____
☐ _____

tasks to-do

☐ _____
☐ _____
☐ _____
☐ _____
☐ _____
☐ _____

_____
_____
_____
_____
_____

project	
deadline	completed ☐

items required

☐ _____
☐ _____
☐ _____
☐ _____
☐ _____
☐ _____

tasks to-do

☐ _____
☐ _____
☐ _____
☐ _____
☐ _____
☐ _____

_____
_____
_____
_____
_____

Project to complete

project	
deadline	completed ☐

items required

tasks to-do

project	
deadline	completed ☐

items required

tasks to-do

Project to complete

project	
deadline	completed ☐

items required

tasks to-do

project	
deadline	completed ☐

items required

tasks to-do

Project to complete

project	
deadline	completed ☐

items required

- ☐
- ☐
- ☐
- ☐
- ☐
- ☐

tasks to-do

- ☐
- ☐
- ☐
- ☐
- ☐
- ☐

project	
deadline	completed ☐

items required

- ☐
- ☐
- ☐
- ☐
- ☐
- ☐

tasks to-do

- ☐
- ☐
- ☐
- ☐
- ☐
- ☐

Project to complete

project	
deadline	completed ☐

items required

tasks to-do

project	
deadline	completed ☐

items required

tasks to-do

Project to complete

project	
deadline	completed ☐

items required   tasks to-do

project	
deadline	completed ☐

items required   tasks to-do

Project to complete

project	
deadline	completed ☐

items required

☐
☐
☐
☐
☐
☐

tasks to-do

☐
☐
☐
☐
☐
☐

project	
deadline	completed ☐

items required

☐
☐
☐
☐
☐
☐

tasks to-do

☐
☐
☐
☐
☐
☐

Project to complete

project	
deadline	completed ☐

items required

tasks to-do

project	
deadline	completed ☐

items required

tasks to-do

Project to complete

project	
deadline	completed ☐

items required | tasks to-do

project	
deadline	completed ☐

items required | tasks to-do

Project to complete

project	
deadline	completed ☐

items required   tasks to-do

project	
deadline	completed ☐

items required   tasks to-do

Project to complete

project	
deadline	completed ☐

items required

tasks to-do

project	
deadline	completed ☐

items required

tasks to-do

Project to complete

project	
deadline	completed ☐

items required

tasks to-do

project	
deadline	completed ☐

items required

tasks to-do

Project to complete

project	
deadline	completed ☐

items required

tasks to-do

project	
deadline	completed ☐

items required

tasks to-do

Project to complete

project	
deadline	completed ☐

items required	tasks to-do

☐
☐
☐
☐
☐
☐

project	
deadline	completed ☐

items required	tasks to-do

☐
☐
☐
☐
☐
☐

Project to complete

project	
deadline	completed ☐

items required

tasks to-do

project	
deadline	completed ☐

items required

tasks to-do

Project to complete

project	
deadline	completed ☐

items required

tasks to-do

project	
deadline	completed ☐

items required

tasks to-do

Project to complete

project	
deadline	completed ☐

items required

tasks to-do

project	
deadline	completed ☐

items required

tasks to-do

Project to complete

project	
deadline	completed ☐

items required   tasks to-do

☐ _____   ☐ _____
☐ _____   ☐ _____
☐ _____   ☐ _____
☐ _____   ☐ _____
☐ _____   ☐ _____
☐ _____   ☐ _____

_____
_____
_____
_____

project	
deadline	completed ☐

items required   tasks to-do

☐ _____   ☐ _____
☐ _____   ☐ _____
☐ _____   ☐ _____
☐ _____   ☐ _____
☐ _____   ☐ _____
☐ _____   ☐ _____

_____
_____
_____
_____

Project to complete

project	
deadline	completed ☐

items required

☐ _____
☐ _____
☐ _____
☐ _____
☐ _____
☐ _____

tasks to-do

☐ _____
☐ _____
☐ _____
☐ _____
☐ _____
☐ _____

_____
_____
_____
_____

project	
deadline	completed ☐

items required

☐ _____
☐ _____
☐ _____
☐ _____
☐ _____
☐ _____

tasks to-do

☐ _____
☐ _____
☐ _____
☐ _____
☐ _____
☐ _____

_____
_____
_____
_____

Project to complete

project	
deadline	completed ☐

items required

tasks to-do

project	
deadline	completed ☐

items required

tasks to-do

www.ingramcontent.com/pod-product-compliance
Lightning Source LLC
Chambersburg PA
CBHW030718220526
45463CB00005B/2100